# Each One, Teach One

by Dr. Annette L. Chambers-Dwyer

DORRANCE
PUBLISHING CO
EST. 1920
PITTSBURGH, PENNSYLVANIA 15238

Dorrance Publishing Co
585 Alpha Drive
Suite 103
Pittsburgh, PA 15238
Visit our website at *www.dorrancebookstore.com*

ISBN: 978-1-6495-7175-5
eISBN: 978-1-6495-7684-2

# Each One, Teach One

# Acknowledgements

At this time, I am proud that I was able to visit the holy land with my mother, Myrtle Chambers, as well as, my former pastor, Rev. Dr. Daniel. Thanks to my husband, Dennis Dwyer, who supported me on this venture and we continue to celebrate our love.

# Introduction

Fernando Cabrera, otherwise known as, Rev. Dr. Cabrera worked as a counselor at Mt. Vernon High School. As a secretary, we worked together by interviewing high school students as I prepared their transcripts for higher education. Dr. Cabrera and his wife were very diligent in uniting Dennis and Annette Dwyer in holy matrimony. As a professor, Fernando has taught many students at Mercy College and is very active in the Bronx districts in bringing about change in lives of their children and grandchildren.

Fernando Cabrera

Tiger woods, one of the best golf players in the United States history was empowered and influenced by his father who was also a golf player. Tiger thought of himself as black and Asian (mixed race); his father being black (colored) and his mother Asian (oriental). Tiger Woods has won many golf tournaments and has faced many challenged while doing so.

Harry Belafonte, West Indian musician, who sun one of the world's favorite songs "Day oh" as well as, "Shake, Shake, Shake, Senora," and many other folk music has influenced me musically, as well as the West Indian Community. We continue to celebrate Harry Belafonte as we reflect on the happiness and healing that he has brought to many people including myself during the pandemic.

In addition, my children: Keri-Ann Dwyer, Desiree Dwyer and Deniece Dwyer are so proud of me and we try to interact with each other the best way possible.

My brothers; Dennis Lawrence and Everton Patrick are proud of me as their younger sister. My sisters and I continue to celebrate each other and have bonded more whenever we are free to meet and fellowship with each other.

To God be the glory!

Dr. Annette L. Chambers-Dwyer
Educator/Author

November 14, 2019

# Just in Time...Time for Change

**It was a beautiful day, one summer day in 2008:** the day I decided to step out in faith as I left my place of employment. Yes, I can clearly remember the institution located in the Bronx. The air felt cool and light as I walked home with a refreshing feeling from the light rain as it drizzled over my face and rain gear. As I walked home, I was assured by God that the decision I made was the best one.

Working with the inner-city children was very rewarding, however, the restrictions, the workload, and the treatment of teachers seemed so unfair.

It was definitely a turnaround moment: one in which I knew that God would make a change—a change that would be beneficial to all. A moment of reflection, a moment of awareness would lead to endless possibilities as I earned a doctorate degree in instructional leadership.

Yes! Yes! I did it! In spite of all the distractions that seemed would turn things "upside down," the still small voice told me, "My child, hold your head up high. It's time for you to shine." Guess what? I believed that voice, the voice of God, that guided me and took me through many meandering roads, ups and downs, twists and turns.

It was 2008, at a church school program in the Wakefield area of the Bronx. There, I met a lovely female pastor named T. Anne Daniel, whom God allowed to enrich, empower, enlighten, and bring about change in the spiritual lives of individuals—including myself—who were lacking in some areas of spiritual, financial, emotional, or psychological aspects of our lives. I would say she is a "phenomenal woman," according to the words of Maya Angelou. She is a woman full of energy and vitality, highly motivated, bold and abrasive, compassionate and loving, and at the same time, very humble.

Through my eyes, she is a great role model: an individual to be admired (like my mother, Myrtle), as she cuddles the little babies and kisses them, as she kisses and blesses us, embodying the agape love that is so pure, but which sometimes can be interpreted differently by others who do not understand God's love.

The year was 2008, the time when Barack Obama was elected as the first black president of the United States. What an achievement!

Better yet, God allowed me to make a change, which I considered challenging, so as to activate my gifts and talents by mentoring church school students, as well as being a part of the Mass choir. It was my former pastor, Rev. Dr. Allen Pinckney Jr., whom I reencountered at Butler Memorial United Methodist Church. At an early age, I found him to be charming, very funny, and caring to individuals, especially children. He is an individual who is very humble but, at the same time, very loving: a "behind-the-scenes kind of guy" who exerts discipline in a very calm manner, that is very crispy clear to individuals.

God allowed me to encounter two loving pastors exercising their warmth, love, and strong desire to see the church grow and prosper, all while making disciples of Christ! What an incredible assignment!

The Rev. Dr. T. Anne Daniel, former pastor, has been known to me for approximately thirteen years. In 2008, I met Rev. Daniel as soon as I returned from Sarasota, Florida and heard that she was preaching at Wakefield Grace United Methodist Church. I said to myself, “Hhhmmm, a woman preacher.” For some strange reason, I started doing a case study (a detailed evaluation) of her to see how effective her preaching was.

As I listened to her preaching from week to week, I became more and more interested in hearing her messages. Again, I said to myself, "Rev. Daniel sounds like a school teacher." She has a sophisticated way of incorporating the Word of God with historical and geographical information to make her messages more in-depth, meaningful, relatable, and understandable. "What a genius!" I would say to myself. Dr. Daniel is also a very inviting individual. She has a way of involving you in activities even if you are not quite ready.

After completing Bible Study II with Rev. Daniel, I can clearly remember as she called on me to share my experience with the Bible study group in order to share in front of the church congregation. I became petrified as she called on me to share. The following day we had to share in front of the church, but when she overlooked me, I said, "Yes, she didn't remember me." Immediately, someone said, "Annette didn't share as yet." I started feeling a little nervous and sweaty. You know I had to do it; I could not argue with her, she is my mentor. During my other bible study classes (III and IV), Rev. Daniel was again the facilitator. She was always punctual, setting a great example for us to follow.

My relationship actually began approximately thirteen years ago after taking over several educational projects at Wakefield Grace United Methodist Church under the leadership of The United Methodist City Society. The mentoring/tutoring program (METOM) was directed by me due to my availability at that time. In addition, Vacation Bible School began in 2009 as a two- week pilot program under the direction of Chery Walfall-Flagg, Vacation Bible School coordinator. I became the Vacation Bible School director.

Several youth—as well as adult volunteers—participated in facilitating the programs, and we developed a good working relationship. I communicated with the Rev. Daniel the progress and concerns of the programs, concerns of volunteers, and my personal challenges. She was very willing, dependable, loving, caring, understanding, and a very easy-to-talk-to individual who listened attentively and responded in a timely manner. Whenever there was a need and she could help, she would respond immediately to satisfy the individual(s). She is very compassionate, always looking out for the youth and children who had various types of disabilities, including my daughter Desiree Dwyer.

Dr. Daniel took the initiative to involve the youth in mission trips to Ghana, Cambodia, and other countries and families in need. One of my other daughters, Deniece Dwyer, was blessed to attend one of the trips to Ghana.

Just in time…I must say, Jesus is right on time, I learned. Jesus is on time in changing my life and the lives of those around me and giving us "new birth" so I could experience God's love in every area of my life. He has taken the wrong and made it right, changing the darkness into light, raising the valleys and peering down the mountains, providing a way to incorporate individuals into a diversified culture, setting the tone for a world of mixed beauty and culture...so phenomenal.

Even more precious is the love that my daughter Desiree and I received among our new church home: the love that is warm and welcoming by several sisters and brothers, a love of inclusion, that allows us to be more open so as to discover our gifts and talents and use them to the glory of God and make an impact on others.

It is this agape love that allows me to rise every day and follow the path that God leads to restore all that the enemy has stolen. This love allows me to interact with children, giving them a chance that I also received: a chance to express themselves in a clear voice. At this moment, God has allowed me the chance to mentor students through the R. Farrell Learning Enrichment Center program to use my gifts and talents. In addition, God is allowing me to be a role model for children through music, reading, and advising. It's so remarkable! God is allowing me to use my gifts and talents to mold children and young adults and prepare them for this challenging life to make disciples for him.

Today, I must say, I have experienced the interactions of the diverse cultures within the charter schools in the North and South Bronx that are doing a tremendous job in fulfilling some of the needs of the children and adults. Praise God!

In 2011, my mother, Myrtle Chambers, decided to go on a trip to the Holy Land under the leadership of Rev. Dr. Daniel. I heard about the trip, and as the time was approaching for the trip, I felt a deep desire to go on that adventure. It was a difficult decision for me to go because my funds were limited. However, I felt the urge and anxiety and decided to go a few months before the date.

As I can recall, it was a spectacular event as we journeyed to the Holy Land from Sunday, February 12, 2012 through Sunday, February 26, 2012. As I reflect on this experience, powerful words come to my mind: "majestic," "awesome," "splendid," "sovereign," "overwhelming," breathtaking moment.

We traveled to Milan in Italy; Olympia in Greece; Israel (Jerusalem, Galilee, and Capernaum); Turkey (Miletus, Ephesus); Greece (Athens); then back to Rome, Italy.

Our first place visited was Milan, Italy where we spent the day going through customs and boarded the ship to Greece. We traveled by bus to Olympia, Greece.

This great landmark consisted of buildings and monuments dating back to 7000 BC, and it was being remodeled and reconstructed to preserve for generations to come. Olympia is known for its great interest in archaeology and athletic competitions. The apostle, Paul, was very inspired by the games which included wrestling, running, and other types of gymnastic activities. Games would be held every four years starting from 776 BC. The last game was held and closed down by 390 AD. The people that live there are called Hellenists. Greece is known to have twelve gods, with their main god being Zeus. Their belief is that these gods serve different purposes—for example, they believe the god of fertility provides rain to keep the land fertile. The land of Greece is very fertile and verdant, gets a lot of rainfall, and produces crops such as lemons, oranges, and vegetables.

As we traveled, we entered Jerusalem. The scenery was magnificent. It consisted of green rolling plains and mountains giving an aura of peace, tranquility, and calm. We saw acres and acres of green fertile land with many olive trees. Biblical reference was made by our tour guide about Moses and the seven fruits: pomegranates, dates, olives, figs, wheat, barley, and grapes.

As time went by, I became frustrated after witnessing the challenges that the pastor had to endure even though she was doing such a splendid job in pastoring the congregation.

My vision became evident as I reflected on what God had done in my life, how he sent a beautiful pastor my way to undo the damages done by a school district, school principal, and coworkers. I was in awe! What a difference in comparison to my former supervisor. I asked myself, "Is she real?" I asked Pastor Daniel, "Are you my friend?" She said "No, I am your pastor." I shared with her that God told me I will be experiencing newness in my life. Many other positive changes started happening. As time went by, my daughter Desiree, whom she prayed for (as well as for myself and members of my family), healing started taking place. As I received more of God's blessings, I got really excited and shared almost everything with Rev. Daniel, via (hundreds of) emails. She was the only teacher/preacher that could fully understand the challenges which God changed into joy, peace, and happiness.

Anne is a very thorough, firm, detail-oriented individual filled with a lot of zeal and zest as she focuses on her mission ahead, which is serving our Lord and Savior, Jesus Christ. She is very trust-worthy, open, willing, honest, and truthful especially if she doesn't agree with you. Our pastor is a very alert individual who is very gifted and talented also. She is excellent at delegating tasks and is provoked if they are not done on time. Rev. Daniel proclaims the truth of God in a very timely fashion, and her actions are aligned with the Word of God. She is one in a million. I will always be grateful to the Rev. Dr. Daniel, my former pastor, for sharing such love, laughter, and compassion with everyone.

Sis. Dr. Annette L. Chambers-Dwyer

# The Beautiful Black Woman of Solidarity

She enters the room with such grace and humility
Saying "hi, how are you?" Showing her hospitality
Strutting through the aisle, the hall, and sanctuary
As she smiles to herself, "Is This All About Me?"
Greeting the members and children with such magnetic personality
"How are you doing?" Sending a message of sincere inner love
Extending the love of God to humanity.

Faced with animosity, she walks a thin line
Trying to create peace, love, and unity so we can be one of a kind.
She adjusts herself, asking, "should I smile today?"
But somehow senses the feeling, hhhmmmm, today is not the day.
So she journeys throughout the groups and committees
Trying to be the best that she can be
Giving a part of herself, but told subtly
You are not a part of this society
Then she peeks, tests, screens, analyzes and finds
That some people do not incorporate her.
She asks again, "What is the aura that they sense in me?"
"How can I really be me if I have to please everybody?"
Guess what? God finally answered and said
"My child, this is not about you, it's about who I want you to be."
So God fashioned, sculpted, carved, and made her over
To suit his purpose, the purpose of eternity.
Now when they ask her "who are you?" She can safely say,
"I am God's child." "Yes," that's me
Predominantly black, white, and Cherokee
Takes care of children due to my magnetic personality
Jamaican, English, African-American, Scottish

They are all parts of my diversity
They ask, are you from the ghetto? She answers,
No, not really, but I am from all other levels of society
Instilled with great morals, standards and values
Just striving for prosperity
They question, what is your profession?
She answers, I am Annie, girl of few trades;
Teacher, musician, poet, author, professor, woman of technology
A child of God, full of strength and vitality
Defender of justice, endorser of revolutionists;
Martin Luther, Nelson Mandela, Barack Obama, Bob Marley
Thinkers, innovators, progressors, just like her.

Well-rounded individual; speaks fluently, interacts intimately, expresses honestly,
Addresses directly, focuses intently, answers intelligently, moves graciously,
Cuddles gently, walks smoothly, dresses modestly, loves naturally.
Gives some of her time, love, and talent to those in need while celebrating God's beauty
So why do you question my integrity, ability, and humanity
If this poem does not apply to you, please don't take it personally,
God is working on us spiritually, intellectually, socially, and economically
What else do you want to know about me? God is working to set us all free…

Amen

# Empowerment - Each One, Teach One, Then Reach One...

**The Harlem Renaissance was a period of change**—awakening, rebirth, and revival of art, music, and literature by not only African Americans, but also Caribbean Americans who saw the need to express themselves intelligently to create a more civilized society by incorporating the different cultures and talents of the people.

This movement, the Harlem Renaissance, began in the 1920s as the New Negro Movement. A large population of blacks from Africa, the Caribbean, and the south migrated to the United States during a period when segregation was at its peak. Blacks were not allowed to integrate with whites. Rosa Parks was told to go to the back of the bus. Ruby Bridges had to be escorted to school. Dionne Warwick, Bill Cosby, Diana Ross, and Smokey Robinson are a few examples of blacks in America who faced injustice but worked diligently to become successful.

Despite the challenges faced by us as a people of color, some of us have risen to a higher level of consciousness to try to undo some of the damages that America faced. Harlem, located on 135th Street and Seventh Avenue, produced a diverse "melting pot" of Afro-Caribbean Americans who rose and demonstrated their talent to effect change that impacted others around the world.

The following are individuals who brought about positive change, in my opinion: Oprah Winfrey, Harry Belafonte, Dionne Warwick, Tracee Ellis Ross, Wynton Marsalis, Barack Obama, Usain Bolt, Senator Fernando Cabrera, Senator Jamaal Bailey, Madam C.J. Walker, Barbra Streisand, Kevin Riley, and many others.

Dr. Howard Gardner sought to enhance the learning skills of children through the different types of intelligence that sparked creativity in students in order for them to discover their type of intelligence. Howard Gardner felt that children learned through different types of intelligences—namely, linguistic, logical-mathematical, spatial, interpersonal, intrapersonal, kinesthetic, musical, naturalistic, and existential intelligence—to express instinctual feelings.

All these types of intelligence are innate (as well as learned) behaviors, however, sometimes we are not aware of them. It takes someone like Dr. Gardner to help us to discover and tap into our innate spirit and use them to praise God the creator.

## Frederick Douglass

**FREDERICK DOUGLASS WAS BORN IN FEBRUARY 1818,** as a slave. At the age of twenty, he escaped slavery and became an anti-slavery activist. During his career, he worked as an abolitionist, author, and photographer. As a photographer, he captured moments during his life that reflected who he was.

His main purpose was to speak against racism and slavery; he was a voice of hope for his people. Douglass was impacted by several people that he worked with. Amy and Isaac Post worked with Douglass on an advisory committee in order to assist runaway slaves. Garrison mentored Douglass and appointed him as an agent of the Massachusetts Anti-Slavery Society; they did many speeches together. They drifted apart because Garrison felt that Douglass didn't show enough empathy for Garrison who was ill. Frederick Douglass died on February 20, 1895.

## Marcus Mosiah Garvey

**MARCUS MOSIAH GARVEY, OTHERWISE KNOWN AS "BLACK MOSES,"** was born August 17, 1887 in St. Ann's Bay, Jamaica and was later married to Amy Jacques Garvey. During his early childhood, Garvey attended school until age fourteen; he taught himself to read and write.

Marcus got involved in many career opportunities, such as Jamaican Political leader, journalist, entrepreneur, and leader of the black nationalist movement. He founded the *Negro World* newspaper and the United Negro Improvement Association (UNIA) in Harlem, NY to unite people of African origin in order to establish their own country.

## Maya Angelou

**MAYA ANGELOU, ALSO KNOWN AS MARGUERITE ANNIE JOHNSON,** was born in St. Louis, Missouri on April 4, 1928. She has been a great icon not only to the American society, but also to the world at large. Her mother, Vivian Baxter, worked several jobs; she was a nurse and car dealer in a casino. Her father, Bailey Johnson, worked as a doorman at an apartment building.

Maya's earlier years was not the typical childhood years. Her parents had challenges; one was the inability to take care of their children, and as a result, her parents divorced when Maya was three years old. As a result, both Maya and her brother, Bailey Jr., were sent to Stamps, Arkansas and were parented by her paternal grandmother. As Maya grew, she became very aware of her surroundings. During her teen years, Maya was raped. Maya became pregnant during her senior year in high school. Despite her challenges of having a baby, she was able to stay in school and graduate by age seventeen. In order to care for her child, Maya worked several jobs. She worked as a cable car conductor, a dancer, a poet, a singer, an actress, and a writer. She married several times; however, due to her traveling and busy schedule, she also spent a lot of time on her career.

Her achievement started skyrocketing after publishing her first volume of her autobiography, *I Know Why the Caged Bird Sings*. One of her poetry books, *Phenomenal Woman*, allowed us to examine her character traits as a successful businesswoman who empowered many African Americans as well as African Caribbean women with her sassy poem, “Still I Rise.” Rising to fame and fortune, Maya Angelou was blessed by working with two well-known icons: the Rev. Dr. Martin Luther King Jr., as well as Malcolm X. Maya received several awards for her outstanding performances, including a Tony nomination for the Broadway play *Look Away* in 1973. Her Pulitzer Prize, awarded in 1972, was one of the highest honors for her poetry book *Just Give Me a Cool Drink of Water 'fore I Diiie*.

Many of her works plummeted Maya’s spirit. In 1993, she was also honored to read her poem at the inauguration of the former president, Bill Clinton. The poem was titled “On the Pulse of Morning.” In 2010, Maya was blessed by former president Barack Obama, who presented her with the Presidential Medal of Freedom.

Maya’s message in her several genres has taught us to embrace each other’s diversity. Her life experience has also influenced us to rise from hardship to a more meaningful life. Most importantly, Maya’s message is about love, hope, and courage shared by the love of Jesus Christ. One of her quotes states, “I’ve learned that people will forget what you said, people will forget you did, but people will never forget how you made them feel.”

Maya has been celebrated in her book *A Celebration of Rising Joy!*. Even though Maya passed away on May 28, 2014, her memory still lives on. She inspired Oprah Winfrey through her cooking and her many talents.

## Oprah Winfrey

**OPRAH, A REMARKABLE WOMAN, POSSESSES LINGUISTIC INTELLIGENCE,** as displayed through her book club. As an actress, Oprah was featured in several movies including *The Color Purple*, which portrayed some challenges faced by African-Americans. As a talk show host and ambassador, Oprah was born on January 29, 1954, and she grew up in Kosciusko, Mississippi. She grew up with her parents, Vernon Winfrey and Vernita Lee. Her parents separated, and Oprah and her mother lived with her grandmother on a small farm. At that time, her grandmother boiled water to wash clothes. As a little girl, Oprah spent six years with her grandmother whom she called Momma. Oprah was taught to read the Bible. She recited verses at the Faith United Mississippi Baptist Church.

Living a difficult life, Oprah went through some social and emotional problems and overcame some of them by reading and dreaming about her future. Oprah was the youngest African American reporter for WTVF-TV in Nashville.

She starred in several shows and movies—namely, "The Oprah Winfrey Show" and *The Color Purple*. Oprah possesses interpersonal skills; she inspired individuals including Dr. Phil, Dr. Oz, and many other doctors of education including myself and my four daughters to rise despite the challenges that might hamper us as people of color.

As with many working families, Oprah was nurtured by her grandmother, Hattie Mae Lee, mother of Vernita Lee, Oprah's mother. Oprah had conflicts with her mother due to the fact that her mother had to work to help support her. As a young girl, Oprah was faced with peer pressure because her clothing was different from the clothes other children had.

At the age of fourteen, Oprah Winfrey went to live with her father in Tennessee where life was less challenging. His intention was for her to get good grades, work on her school assignments, and read one book per week and respond to the literature. To me, that was fascinating! Even more fascinating was the fact that Oprah was influenced by Maya Angelou's autobiography, *I Know Why The Caged Bird Sings*. Oprah could truly relate, as well as many of us Black women, to not only the struggle, but also the change.

Oprah Winfrey interacted with individuals through the media, as well as through churches to reach millions around the world through "The Oprah Winfrey Show." After working in the classroom in the Bronx, New York, I would rush home to watch the show.

## Dr. Martin Luther King Jr.

**The Rev. Dr. Martin Luther King Jr. was a peacemaker who** wanted blacks, whites, and people of other races to integrate with each other so that in time we would all be free. He influenced many people through his speech "I Have a Dream." Today, in the year 2020, we have made significant progress. However, the struggle still continues. The year 2020 we encountered a pandemic which caused a turmoil in our lives; electing President Biden and Kamala Harris brought forth a "breath of fresh air."

## Wynton Marsalis

**WYNTON LEARSON MARSALIS WAS BORN OCTOBER 18, 1961 TO** Ellis and Dolores Marsalis, among six sons. He possesses musical intelligence, as shown in his performances in New York City. Wynton is a trumpeter who composes, teaches, and directs at Lincoln Center. His area of expertise is performing classical and jazz music catering to young audiences. He attended Benjamin Franklin High School, as well as The Juilliard School. At the age of fourteen, Wynton performed at the Fairview Baptist Church with several jazz bands including the New Orleans Youth Orchestra, New Orleans Symphony, and New Orleans Community Concert Band. Wynton, at the age of seventeen, became the youngest musician admitted to Tanglewood's Berkshire Music Center. He was awarded the Harvey Shapiro Award and moved to New York City to attend Juilliard in 1979. Starting in 1981, Wynton performed over 120 concerts over a period of fifteen years.

Wynton produced over eighty records, selling over seven million copies. These recordings include jazz, blues, and swing. In 2009, Marsalis' Blues Symphony was incorporated with ragtime rhythms by Atlanta Symphony Orchestra, creating a classical repertoire expanded to include Swing Symphony.

*The Jungle*, a musical portrait of New York City, was performed in December 2016. In July 2017, the Jazz at Lincoln Center and the New York Philharmonic reunited to present *The Jungle* in Shanghai. Wynton was awarded the Pulitzer Prize for music, the Grammy Award for Best Improvised Jazz Solo, and the NAACP Image Award for outstanding Jazz Album.

Marsalis' rich, cultural music categorized him among the world's most significant composers.

## Barack Obama

**Barack Obama, husband of Michelle Obama and father of** Sasha and Malia Obama, was the forty-fourth president of the United States. The contributions he made have surpassed many former presidents. He has made significant impressions on the world.

In 2006, as I was shopping in Costco, I came across a book entitled *The Audacity of Hope: Thoughts on Reclaiming the American Dream*. On the cover was a picture of Barack Obama whom I heard would be running for president in 2008. Immediately, I told myself that he would be the first African American president, and guess what? He did it. As I researched Barack, I realized that he was born in the same year I was. I relayed this information to my husband, children, and grandchildren. We were all happy and excited for him.

Barack Obama served for eight years, accompanied by his wife Michelle Obama and children Sasha and Malia. There were many challenges as they tried to pass laws concerning healthcare, educational challenges, and many more issues in Congress. He overcame many obstacles which brought about many positive changes in society and around the world. As of today, we have achieved much. However, the struggle still continues under the leadership of President Donald Trump…

## President Donald Trump

**Donald Trump was the 45th president of the United States,** and he has used some of the ideas of former president Barack Obama while implementing his own. Many changes are occurring in our society—some are positive, but others are negative. American families—in the churches, schools, and society—are trying to make sense of what is happening. The true realization is that everyone is trying to use their "nature" and "nurture" talents to keep hope alive.

## The Real TV Program

**"The Real" is a television program that is very enlightening** and empowering, not only to me, but also to many people around the world. The television program has broadened my education and extended my scope and view of current happenings as we are all looking forward to achieving and learning ways to cope with our vast cultural differences. The crew includes six women, namely,

Tamera Mowry-Housley, Loni Love, Amanda Seales, Garcelle Beauvais, Adrienne Houghton, and Jeannie Mai. My husband, Dennis Dwyer, my four beautiful girls, and I have watched the show "Sister, Sister" as the twins have grown to be mothers of their own children, and we are so fascinated by their talents. Adrienne Houghton has grown up also on several television shows, including "Power Puff Girls" and "Showtime at the Apollo" with Steve Harvey. Loni, who is an engineer, has broadened her horizons by using her knowledge to impress others in many areas of her life. These six women possess the talent of not only interacting with each other, but also with the Americans and people around the world; they have brought incredible love and experience to many audiences and communities. I truly enjoy their jovial entertainment. As a teacher who taught in the Yonkers, Mt. Vernon, and New York City districts, I can attest to the struggle of teachers in the classroom. As a professor within the City University of New York, I realize that the struggle still continues.

Teachers and professors who have paved the way for many children and adults need to have financial compensation for their progressive work in educating individuals in their professional arenas.

## Duke Ellington

**Edward Kennedy, also known as Duke Ellington,** was born on April 29, 1899. He was a composer, pianist, and bandleader. His musical revues included *Sophisticated Ladies*, and another of his popular musical masterpieces is "Take the A Train." He was such a musical genius.

## Usain Bolt

**Usain St. Leo Bolt, nicknamed "lightning bolt,"** was born August 21, 1986 in Sherwood Content, Trelawny, Jamaica. He attended William Knibb Memorial High School. At the Beijing Summer Olympic Games in 2008, Usain won three gold medals. He is a Jamaican sprinter known to be the fastest human being, completing 200 meters in twenty seconds.

## "Smokey" Robinson

**William "Smokey" Robinson Jr. (born February 19, 1940) is** an American singer, songwriter, record producer, and former record executive. Robinson was the founder and frontman of the Motown vocal group the Miracles.

## Beres Hammond

**Beres Hammond, who also possesses musical intelligence,** was born on August 28, 1955. As a Jamaican reggae singer, Beres is known for his lovers rock music. He wrote many songs including "I Feel Good" and "What One Dance Can Do." He is a great musical icon.

## Mae Carol Jemison

**Mae Carol Jemison is an American engineer, physician,** and NASA astronaut. She became the first African American woman to travel in space. She went into orbit aboard the space shuttle *Endeavor* on September 12, 1992.

## Alicia Keyes

**Alicia Keyes, also known as Alicia Augello Cook,** is an African American singer, songwriter, pianist, and actress. Alicia Keyes released her debut album with J Records, after first having record deals with Columbia Arista Records. Alicia is known as a woman of mixed race. She expresses her diversity by interacting with many races through movies and songs.

As an educator in both the Westchester School district and the New York City school district, I have witnessed many challenges, growth of students, and changes in the church and school curriculum that have allowed some of our students to flourish though some are still struggling. As a part of the education team at Lehman College – City University of New York (CUNY), I can say amazing things are happening.

Annette L. Dwyer, EdD
Author/Doctor of Education

**Drawing 6**

**Drawing 7**

**Drawing 8**

CPSIA information can be obtained
at www.ICGtesting.com
Printed in the USA
LVHW071042190422
716440LV00022B/4

* 9 7 8 1 6 4 9 5 7 1 7 5 5 *